Phenomenal Woman

Poetry Anthology

Collection of poems in honour of Maya Angelou
Written by a league of great poetic minds
across the globe.

Edited by Ifeanyi Enoch Onuoha & Ogwo David Emenike

Powered by Hinovelty

Praises for Dr. Maya Angelou

"One of the brightest lights of our time - a brilliant writer, a fierce friend, and a truly phenomenal woman."
Barack Obama,
44th President of the United States of America

"So, we must carry on and pass on, lifting humanity up, helping people to live lives of purpose and dignity, to pass on the poetry of courage and respect. That is what she would want. That is what we will do."
Oprah Winfrey,
Media Proprietor, Talk Show Host, Actress, Producer, and Philanthropist

"She called our attention in thousands of ways to her belief that life is a gift, manifest in each new day. She called our attention to the fact that the things that really matter - dignity, work, love and kindness - are things we can all share and do not cost anything. And they matter more than the difference of wealth and power, of strength and beauty, of intellect."
Bill Clinton,
42nd President of the United States of America

"A remarkable spirit, a voice for the voiceless, a national treasure whose words inspired millions."
Andre Carson,
United States Congressman

"Maya Angelou served as a lifelong inspiration to all of us. While she has passed, I know her words and her works will continue to live on."
Debbie Stabenow,
United States Senator

The Phenomenal Woman Poetry Anthology
Copyright © 2015: Ifeanyi Enoch Onuoha
& Ogwo David Emenike

ISBN-13: 978-1503012417
ISBN-10: 1503012417

Powered by **Hinovelty**

For inquiries:
Email: hinovelty1@gmail.com
Phone: +2348037633034, +2347036466412

Cover photo by Dwight Carter Photography
Cover design & Book packaging by Hinovelty

Table of Contents

<u>Dedication</u>

This work is a humble dedication to Dr. Maya Angelou. Born Marguerite Annie Johnson, she was an author, poet, philanthropist, civil rights activist, educator, producer, mentor, playwright, singer, actress, director, historian and producer.

Born April 4, 1928 - St. Louis, Missouri, U.S.A.
Died May 28, 2014 - Winston-Salem, North Carolina, U.S.A.

The life and works of Dr. Maya Angelou are living legacies that have influenced and will continue to influence millions of lives.

The epitome of a Phenomenal Woman.

May her lovely soul enjoy bliss in the bosom of God Almighty.

<u>Acknowledgment</u>

Nobody can achieve success alone for teamwork is the secret that makes common people achieve uncommon result. We give all glory to God Almighty for giving us the provisions to make this vision a success.

To all the writers that participated in this project, we salute you greatly for without your contributions, this work would not be a success. We wish you greater success in your endeavors and may your writing continue to inspire lives.

To Tammie Roundtree, Lerato Matsaneng, Chinecherem Kalu, and all members of team Hinovelty, thank you for giving your best to the success of this project.

To the family, mentees, admirers and friends of Dr. Maya Angelou, may God give you the fortitude to bear this loss.

To you dear reader, may the wisdom in this book be a blessing to your life.

Foreword

The honorary responsibility of writing the foreword to this all-important poetry anthology dedicated to a woman of phenomenal achievements, further exposed me to the extraordinary life and times of one whose early years were characterized by "hard nuts" only few would successfully crack and move on in life into attaining sterling pedestals of position references to her people and country, the United States and the world at large. As an African-American who rose from grass to grace, a nobody to somebody of high esteem and influence at a time when racism had the San Francisco authorities 'seal of approval', her story will remain an all-time inspiration to anyone. It simply says; to be focused and steadfast, one could overcome life's hiccups and win medals for oneself in outstanding performances touching on different fields of human endeavor, etc. From the back waters stamps, Arkansas, United States, Maya Angelou, in whose honor this anthology was birthed, became a woman of immense importance whose activities span all spheres of life and impacted positively on millions; every reader would wonder how one who had personal contacts with famous civil rights crusaders like Malcom X, Martin Luther King Jr., etc, was gracefully around till 2014 spreading the virtues of love, and oneness, for the general well-being of humanity. One is encouraged that, selfless deeds will always attract the best of returns in more ways than one now or in the future. Maya Angelou was an epitome of the finest outcomes from the perfect hands of God; a supposed societal dreg becoming a keg and fountain of knowledge from which the world drank and will keep drinking as demonstrated in her extraordinary talents in music, dance and poetry. Writing a foreword on an award-winning autobiographer edges one from writing a 'regular foreword' to an 'autobiographical foreword' but managing the challenges in this regard would see one overcoming the temptation of rehashing her lifetime/activities which space wouldn't permit. As one who bumped into the world of young fathers early in life, I am always touched by stories of others who have passed through similar situations and managing the same to a level where one attracts recognizable attention to deserving the honor of writing a foreword to this anthology as mentioned, is a pleasant twixt/happening whose happenstance will stand etched in my memory. A school drop-out who later went back to school, Maya Angelou was the first female African American cable car conductor, single mother at age 16, waitress and cook, night club singer, who became reputable as an author, poet, Teacher, Lecturer, screen-play writer, film director, actress, singer, and credited with numerous books of poetry, Essays, plays and novels, etc. She had a mind-blowing existence that will send shivers down the spine of anyone encountering the stories of her life and times; rough as it was, she braved, weathered and coasted home as an all-time personality that impacted the world. An autobiographer of esteem repute, her award-winning memoir; "*I know why the caged birds sing*" won her national and international recognitions that saw her speaking to audiences in America and across the world. From President Barack Obama, she received the highest honor any civilian would receive in the United States; the Presidential Medal of Freedom. Of her numerous quotes, the following will interest you; "When members of a society wish to secure that society's rich heritage they cherish their arts and respect their artists. The esteem with which we regard the multiple cultures offered in our country enhances our possibilities for healthy survival and continued social development."

The Phenomenal Woman Poetry Anthology is of sterling traditions and standing as a pillar for the promotion of poetry/literature as a tool for societal progress and development. Phenomenal as her achievements sounded, how many of our leaders, academicians, professionals and the like could tell of her person? It would not be out of place to state that, some contributors to this anthology may know of Maya Angelou only after responding to the call for submission of poems leading to this great poetry anthology. Accordingly, it is expected that, everyone who encounters this book would be inspired to be steadfast and keeping to virtues of hard work, selflessness, dedication and focus to whatever he/she does as well as have unshaken faith in God Almighty.

The Editors of this anthology of poems must be commended for their forthrightness in honoring an extra-ordinary personality in the person of Maya Angelou. There's no doubt that it's a noble venture whose coming is at the nick of time when nations are in dire need of heroes as role models for the re-establishment of men and women downplaying selfishness for selflessness. That contributors were drawn from all over the world testifies of our world as one; one humanity of common objectives of a good life devoid of discrimination and injustice.

Eriata Oribhabor,
Poet, Poetry Promoter, Essayist & Published Author

Editors Note

The phenomenal people in this world are those that relentlessly overcome the challenges of life. They have an ability to ignore the scoffers and turning the seemingly impossible to possible. Dr. Maya Angelou (Marguerite Annie Johnson) was one such great soul. She weathered the storms of life, rose to become a leading light, freeing the caged birds of human potential with her wealth of wisdom - a beautiful and powerful reason to gather in her name.

Your life is an art; make it a masterpiece because every man is the craftsman of his future, whether he hone it himself or allow fate to do it. The sagacity in this book will equip you to position yourself rightly for success. Don't cage yourself and allow life to pass you by, seize it, live it, and enjoy it purposefully. No matter how bad your beginning was, you can make it better, rise from victim to victor, and become a rainbow of hope and a light that lights up lives and places.

The goal of this anthology is in line with one of the visions of Hinovelty, which is to cause a social change that upholds values and uproots vices through the celebration of good role models. Dr. Maya Angelou is an exemplar not just to women but also to men. Through her life and works, she taught us to love one another, work hard, and support good causes that help to move society forward.

In this book, you will enjoy ageless poetry by great writers honoring Dr. Maya Angelou and creatively tailored to inspire you to live a purpose-driven life. The labors of our heroes and sheroes shall never be in vain.

There's something for you in this book, come join us and journey through it and your life will experience a quantum leap into success giving you the key to unlock your greater life, living, and legacy.

- Ifeanyi Enoch Onuoha & Ogwo David Emenike

Disclaimer:

This book contains original work submitted by the authors. There has been no editing of grammar, punctuation, tensing, phrasing, or style of any of the submitted work. This was to ensure the authenticity of the work and the authors' complete freedom of expression.

Authors were requested to submit their work in English, so as to ensure that as many people as possible were able to enjoy this book. Please be advised that English is not the first language of many of the authors and editors of this book.

Minor formatting changes were made in an attempt to ensure consistency across the book.

Chapter 1

Maya Angelou

Photo source: http://bit.ly/1z1zRpB

Maya's Endeavors will Endure
By **Rosemary Onyango**

Like a bird awakened in a lonely cage, you flew out
Bracing yourself to embark on voyages of growth
You tore the veil of silence into shreds and tossed it into the
air
You breathed life into expressions with unique flair
Your rich voice spoke boldly about plain truths
Lingering smiles graced your reassuring face and queenly
poise

You witnessed many historic milestones
Akin to your own unfolding turning points
You may have smelt the era of the Great Depression
When many workers' faces were bedewed
With sweat of fatigue and tears of desperation
For a generation that strived to acquire well-tailored wings
These adversities foreshadowed anticipation

You held roles many would have deemed insurmountable
Gradually, challenging those who disdained you
As speaker, actress, singer, dancer, writer and mother
You modeled that we can rip the seems of labeling
With the sharp blades of sheer determination
In each role you reminded us that social justice matters

Persistently you clinched a craving for catharsis
 Developed a knack of lending poetic panache to ordinary
words
You created your own stories and defined your own
authority
That reminded us not to read all your writing as mere
escapism

Your ink kept flowing into the landscapes of our
consciousness
Inspiring lyrics of hope struck a chord in many listeners
Who felt drawn to the beat of the rhythm of your words

You stood tall and stood up for yourself and others
Your zeal for justice soaked your awakened psyche
Believing that silence and by standing will not protect us
The Civil Rights Movement felt your bold footprints
Your ability to capture moments that others thrust aside
Seeded your metamorphosis that bloomed into a new
incarnation

Although you navigated tumultuous times
Your activism extended beyond your charisma
The success that eluded you in your youth
Did not overwhelm you in maturity
Respectfully, you gained entrée into circles of nobility
Delivering creeds that inspire us to reflect and reevaluate
Yours was a long walk to a well-deserved distinction

Because you soared above life's grinding storms
You seemed to hold a big piece of the sky
That makes us yen to drink deep from your wisdom's
fountain
Like a rainbow, you carried a mantle of a brighter day
That reminds us that we must not lose our ventures
But leave a well-blazed trail for budding brilliance

Rosemary Onyango, a Kenyan, teaches interdisciplinary courses at
Eastern Illinois University, USA.

When I'm Gone

(*Dedicated to Maya Angelou*)
By **Lerato Matsaneng**

When I'm gone
I want you not to cry but to read
Read the words I wrote you
Words that litter your shelves and gather dust, as they
anticipate your desire to want them
Words I was sent here by God to share with you
Words to remind you that you are great
Remind you that You are a Phenomenal Woman and Why
Still You Rise.

When I'm gone
I will leave you with every word I shared with you
You will search the world looking to remember the words,
only to find them inside you
Nestled deep down in your heart between your desire to
love and fear to hate

My words will bridge the gap and remind you to love and
only love
And never to fear.

When I'm gone
I will no longer share my words with you
Because now they are yours to share
Yours to run into the dancing wind with
Yours to decorate the walls of your heart with
Yours to dance a tune to
My words are yours.

My day is done - it's done I bid you farewell
I thank you for making space in your lives to hear my words.
I was borrowed to you only for a time
A time to deliver messages to you
Messages you already knew but needed to rehear
Words of reassurance, strength, love and forgiveness I wrote
many words to you, for you.

God borrowed me to you, to ignite your heart
I walked around in the palm of your hands with no modesty
I paraded my words at my leisure, of which you took notice
of
I never held a gun to you but yet you feared me
Feared the pain, power and love my words would pull from
you
You revelled at my words.

When I'm gone
I will no longer be here to remind you
Remind you to remember to be a Phenomenal Woman
To remind you why the Caged Bird Sings
To remind you why Still You Rise
I was a debt unto you from my maker
The Lord has repaid and now I journey home to my maker.

When I'm gone
I will leave you with lessons
Lessons you have learnt and now should teach
Lessons you need to always remember
Remember to say no when its no
Remember that when someone shows you who they are-
believe them

Remember to be a child of God.

An innocent and pure child of God
Remember to forgive, don't with hold forgiveness even from
those who do not ask for it
Have the willingness to listen
The patience to understand
The strength to support
The heart to care and just to be there.
When I'm gone, I will be gone.

Lerato Matsaneng from Sebokeng, South Africa is a published author and communications professional. Her romance novel, *Love on the Menu*, was published in 2011. She lives by the motto: Live, Laugh, love, and Learn.

Women who made us to be
by **Christena AV Williams**

History may be re-written however, memories are
untouched
The life and Journey of you, others and I will not be
forgotten
The legacy one leaves behind will continue to be written in
various literary forms.
My mother's Journey is vital to my character
My understanding of a woman,
Powerful women especially in history have carved out
virtuousness in me.
I read your poems, I felt the emotion in my soul, and it was
real
You ministered to me and I was moved and transformed by
the letters which you turned into words which was
conveyed as a poem.
Mother, sister, Aunt, cousin
Women of every colour, creed, religion and race is
appreciated
Phenomenal woman that is you- Maya Angelou
May your words continue to be a testimony of your life.

Christena AV Williams is Jamaican born emerging revolutionist, a
renowned poet and author of Pearls Among Stones published by
Canadian, Brian Wixon.

Electric Asphodel
(*homage to Maya Angelou*)
by **Károly Sándor Pallai**

A woman on her knees swinging to and fro
In the hail of existence like a flowery dream,
Like the metalline notes of metaphysical jazz
Sneaking out of the cage through the greyness
Of ill-matched everyday life. Dancing away
The swollen malices, singing the oily smells of
Mystery into the onerous, ungainly daybreak.
Choleric skies smoothing out the hemlock dirges
Of the Missouri lands as the nudity of your
Absence resonates in the vertiginous rhapsody.
Narrative and political affirmation in an autobiographical
Paradise creased under the unswerving march
Of legs crooked in pain. A prayer in front
Of the prancing horse of the night, pallet-words
And gracious fragments of black granite blend
Into a stance of enchanting, smoky and shimmering Truth.
Mephitic memories of a child, a lacerating
Iron haze of ecstasy eating itself through the timorous,
Chaste blouse. Pale eyes cutting across the mute
Screenplays of the years, crying blossoms caressing
The sanguinary wheels of a streetcar : wishes erased
Under the heavy breasts of a crudely fate.
A never-ending legacy of Winston-Salem afternoons,
Branding question marks, aneurismal fissures on our Hearts.
The dusty sunsets still linger here, reminding us
Of the sunflower innocence, of your unwearying dynamos
Coughing peremptory questions of race and identity.
An elapse of a visionary biography, an amaranth

And crimson supplication embracing the clouds.

Károly Sándor Pallai is a Hungarian poet who writes poetry in ten languages. He has published three books; his texts appear regularly in electronic and print reviews worldwide.

My Kind of Phenomenal Woman
by **Elizabeth Esguerra Castillo**

Your words imprint a lasting effect on our minds
The immortal messages still linger in our thoughts
Your intricate and evocative verses
Still echo even in the wilderness.

Your name itself is legendary, angelic
You are my kind of phenomenal woman
A woman of substance, a woman empowering other women
You moved the world with your mighty pen.

You are my kind of phenomenal woman
A great inspiration you have bestowed upon mankind
Even if years would go by, your words will remain forever in
our hearts
For these have become part of our existence.

Elizabeth Esguerra Castillo is a Professional Writer, Journalist and
blogger from the Philippines. She is a poet and author of *Seasons of
Emotions* and *Inner Reflections of the Muse*. She is a member of
American Authors Association (AAA).

The Extraordinary Maya
by **Paul Alowo**

There was an extraordinary woman
Whose literary work eludes description
An African American Queen
Whose recitation culminated
The golden dust of wisdom

She touched the world with her sonorous voice
An unsung heroine that inspired the universe
From far beyond, her words rang clear
Divine truth became her crowning glory

Without shame, she stood for what was right
Shining in her robe of royal tapestry
That beautiful goddess from Heaven
Used her pen to spread across Atlantic

From ocean to shining sea
She ignited the flames of passion
Stirred the gusty winds of inspiration
And stood tall upon earthly pedestals
Touching the world and beyond with love

That undying spirit of compassion
Leaned beyond the chains of sexism and racism
With might, the preached the songs of existence Her truth
was reality far from falsity
With a heart unconcealed
She came, She evolved, She survived all!

Paul Alowo is a rising star in the art of spoken word poetry. He is creative thinker, fine-artist, teacher, and a business educator.

Used and Abused
by **Mamello Keketso Sago**

She carries her tattered pride on her back
Like a shadow that over powers its image
As she walks in the early morning hours
A quick buck was all she had hoped to secure

As she marauds endlessly in the streets
Wishing for her wealth to multiply
She is overpowered by her guilty conscious
That causes doubt of the trade

Known as 'Miss Used and Abused'
Men flock in multitudes to satisfy their needs
Proclaiming their rights over her temple
That is filled with nothing but deposits of multiple orgasms'
They ejaculate and pride themselves with
Calling it validation of their elongated phallic structures

With apparent stains on her attire
She evidently accepts her destructive fate
For her reputation surpasses her, they mock her
As they drop her at the same corner
Torn in-between right and wrong
She realizes herself worth's diminishing status
Yet she knows no way out
For her confessions to God are nothing but a silent scream
That penetrates the depth of her heart
Causing tears of the shattered heart to transcend.
As she dwells in her mental poverty
She is confronted by the lie she leads

Keeping up appearances cause her to feel ashamed
For what it is, is a pure web of self destruction?

As she surrenders on bended knees
And professes words of virtue
Proclaiming her dignity and pride back with assertion.

In deep thought, she smiles
And awaits a new dawn with a new beginning
Like a snake that has shed its skin
For the script has taken another course.

Mamello Keketso Sago from Botswana is a wordsmith who loves the art of painting a canvass with words and thrilled to share her zeitgeist with the world.

Maya Goes Higher
by **Abegunde Sunday Olaoluwa**

I write this paean
In memoriam of a felt poet
An amazon among womankind
Whose impacts I bet is felt
In the world she'd left behind

O' Angelou Maya
The song of the caged bird coinage-r
Whose senescence lured
To board that charabanc
That take legends off the world
To the cairn forest, for rest

Adieu O' Angelou Maya
The song of the caged bird coinage-r
Adieu O' poetic wisdom
Which won U.S Medal of Freedom
Adieu to you bard bird, Angelou
Now soaring high beyond the sparrow
Rejoicing with angels up there
As we run on with your legacy here.

Abegunde Sunday Olaoluwa is a Nigerian-born motivational Consultant of Speaking writer and speaker. He is the author of '*Unleash Your Potential Beyond Just Motivation*' and the Principal Pen International Concept.

A Woman of Essence
by **Dan Saefullah Mustapha**

She is phenomenally enriched
With phenomenal features
To all women of essence she is an astounding teacher
A diva, who walked with the rugged
And dined with the covered
A distinguished character of a woman who washed well her
hands

And so she ate with elders
Whose royalty was crowned
By the blisses of her words
And the royalty of her skin
Her feet crossed the rivers of unity
Her heartbeat sang the praises of peace
And her smiles sparkles the beauty of nature
She is phenomenally enriched
With phenomenal features
Where there is darkness
She is a niche
Where there is light
She is the star that shines
Men sang her praise
And pretty women wished for her place she fought and died
in the line of duty seeking for just one wish
The phenomenal woman
Of the exceptional African beauty
A born queen of genuity
Who trudged on the path dignity
And built a kingdom of a woman' integrity

For she is phenomenally enriched with phenomenal features.

Dan Saefullah Mustapha holds a Bachelor of Arts degree in Religious Studies from Islamic University Ghana; he is a renowned Muslim spoken word Artist and the author of '*the Monument of Faith.*'

She Was
by **Melissa Carruthers-Wilson**

She was an inspiration
Inspiring personal growth and contemplation
Opening a door of intense reflection, causing her to be
immortilized, within the pages of historic expression
An example of the magical creative force of womanhood
So worthy of emulation
She is the embodiment of a prism
Of transparent awareness and
Creative expression
For those of us who search for meaning, beyond the
mundane
And embrace any intellectual enlightenment that we find
A door that is never closed to an open, inquisitive, fertile
mind.

MeLissa is a mother, a poet, freelance journalist, and author of
"Conquering Regret".

Chapter 2

Maya Angelou

Photo source: http://bit.ly/1KdpEaq

Maya - The Phenomenal Muse
by **Anurag A Sharma**

I saw her in a dream
And an angel of bright wings
Protecting her virtuous mind
As a guardian of heaven's bliss
Since for humanity she was engaged,
But for that day I didn't wait
When the angel murmured in fair tone
'Now God wants to protect you as her own'
And the next day whole world was alone.

This nature has fostered
Many wits of art, many bright stars
But Even the Stars Look Lonesome
When there is no path of light,
You were the vision of those stars bright.

Also I know Why the Caged Bird Sings,
Perhaps her heavenly notes
Would move the God to free her wings.
Perhaps you were that bird,
Your crispy chimes move all wits, Inspire us your surviving
past That no step is ever the last.

I saw her in a dream
And a beam from the dense clouds
To a beautiful woman's womb
And the same guardian protecting around.

Its yellow, bloomed again in withered tree
Somewhere she has born,
It's buzzing sweet around the tree, Honeybee
Somewhere she has cried in poetic tone,
We are not alone.

Anurag A. Sharma is an Indian born poet and a lover of poetry; he is currently doing a post graduate course in English Language.

Unleash the Hero Within
by **Amaka Imani Nkosazana**

Among everything you set forth to achieve in life
Do so with courage, boldness, and less strife
Let your intuition guide you along the way
Remember words are powerful be careful what you say
Focus your attention on more positivism, be optimistic
Spend less energy on negativity do not be pessimistic
Build your hopes and dreams on everlasting moments And
evaluate yourself to make gradual improvements
At times things may not turn out like you'd expect
Never doubt yourself because you deserve utmost respect

Life has many obstacles and sometimes you must build a
bridge
Challenging yourself should not hinder consider it a privilege
Anger and frustration weakens you giving lead way to doubt
Uphold your values amid the confusion to figure it all out
Dreams become reality once removed from your
imagination
And put into actions, then you come to the realization
That everything conceived began as a thought towards
development
You were created for a purpose and programmed with an
assignment
Just like the sun, planet, moon, and stars are in perfect
alignment

Each day is an opportunity for you to share great inspiration
Every second, minute, hour of the day is your invitation

Move forward in your life there is no time for
procrastination
Understand truth and steer clear from all infatuation
Don't neglect your future by focusing on events in your past
Pace yourself for the race and you discover you are first not
last
Many came before you and proved that it can definitely be
done
You are unique and special unlike no other, the only one
So when you have a promising dream or unrelenting desire
Let no one extinguish your flames or put out your burning
fire
You have good moral character and wisdom to teach and
inspire

Amaka Imani Nkosazana is a published author and poet. She dedicates a majority of her time inspiring others to live their dreams. Amaka is a fond believer that anything is possible through faith.

.

Super Woman
by **Sanni Oluwole**

I have never met you
But have met your good name
I have never seen your beautiful eyes
But your legacies are glued to my forehead
I have never shaken your hands
But have been shaken by your quotes
I have never adored you
But here is the only way to do so.
Thank you for pouring out all your ingenuities!

Sanni Oluwole was born in Ibadan, Nigeria. He is currently on his
National Youth Service Corps Scheme in Kwara State, Nigeria.

Maya
by **Bob McNeil**

Abuse muted
her vocal wellspring.
In that inexpressible Hell,
Maya understood birds held behind metal.

Exploring her circumstance,
she advanced
and discovered ways of recovering
her fortitude.

No longer at an imperceptible decibel,
she uttered tutorials
that helped spiritualize our trails.

Maya published our wishes.
Her books birthed our ambitions.
Today, we, Angelou's orphans,
use humbled keypads
and type tributes to her gospel.

Bob McNeil was influenced by Maya Angelou. Furthermore, even after many years of being a professional illustrator, orator and writer, he still hopes to address the needs of the world.

A True Woman
by **N.K. David**

A phenomenal woman
With a brave and startling truth
Oh! You are a mother: a cradle to hold me
For your sake I shout, mom and me and mom!

You have the heart of love
Hallelujah! You gave hope to the prostitutes and sexually
abused
Now there is a celebration ritual of peace and prayer
For your sake, life doesn't frighten me any more.

You said, "Gather together in my name"
 For your name is a song flung up to heaven
Oh! Shakers, why don't you sing
For now, Sheba sings the song.

Now I hear, "Just give me a cool drink of water for I die"
Oh! Pray my wings are gonna fit me well
And I shall not be moved
For even though I may fall and still I rise.

Not even a black candle
For I wouldn't take nothing for my journey now
Even the stars look lonesome
For although, all God's children need a traveling shoes.

Now, I know why the caged Bird sings
On the pulse of morning
Singing and swinging and getting merry like Christmas

For the phenomenal woman is gone and heaven rejoice for a job well done.

N.K. David is an International Author published author of great books. He stands for justice, equity, and religious tolerance. He is an agent of positive change in modern time and likes making friend with those who share same vision.

One
by **Lennee Reid**

We do not need 10 commandments
Just this one truth
There are no divisions we are one

One mind one body one soul One life one planet just one

So this is my plea this is my cry
If you do not understand I cannot tell you why
It is the ground under my feet
And my eye in the skies

I am one

When you see your brothers and sisters and say
Hey, how ya doing? Are you good?
Remember we are one we all need something

Like the truth in the center of all the spokes in a wheel
Surrounded in hope and love
I honestly see we are one

Black white brown yellow and red
Gay straight queer square
We are all eating from the same plate
And sleeping in one bed

When we think of each other instead of fear
Accept each other as one

When you see a sick puppy
Or a wolf pack on the attack why stay back?

Can't you see we are in one condition
And behave as one?

Look at us and yourself in the mirror
Because everything is one

BECAUSE EVERYTHING IS ONE!

Now who said let there be no divisions among us?
There are none here with one
There are no fences cells prisons or walls
They are all a dream an illusion we are one

I am one

You are one person with one perspective
Born with one will and one tongue
At one time from one mother

Just one

If you seek the truth then you are one
If we'd all love our enemies...
Well I'd guess there would be none!
Are you one?
There are no enemies in one

One mind body soul life planet only one

We are one the Christian Muslim Jew

Animist Humanist Atheist Hindu
Wiccan Pagan the Zen Buddhists too
The agnostics are ahead of me here
You all knew there might be one

And here it is because we are one

Seeking wisdom truth and honesty
Understanding acceptance and forgiveness
Praying meditating and debating

Who has the best answer?
How to attain nirvana?
Will I be accepted in heaven?

Are we really separated by love people?
What are we arguing about?
Whatever it is the answer is we are one

Like one truth in the center of all the spokes in a wheel
Surrounded in hope and love
I honestly believe that we are one

Preacher and sinner one
Cops robbers judges prisoners one
Dealers addicts Bloods Crips hoes and pimps one Soldiers
generals president pope one
Kings queens and refugees
One life love hope dream and one fear
The past the present the future
Right here and now is one

The oppressors and the oppressed one
The rich and the homeless one

In the gutter the mansion the igloo the shack
The tee pee the longhouse wherever ONE is at

I am my temple our temple is we
Let us be at home as one

One peace one hope one wish
In the honor and memory of Martin Luther king
I too have a dream and it is one!

That the separations divisions' denominations indifference
and hate
We have between each other
Is one thing we will get rid of and do without
Where ever when ever and in what ever language
 Truth is spoken in

One father sky one mother earth
All our cultures coming from going to and at one Just like

One truth in the center
Of all the spokes in a wheel Surrounded in hope and love

I honestly believe the truth is
We here all are this one

Lennee Reid is a truth seeker, nature lover, poet and survivor. She is the
mother of one child and lives in Olympia, Washington, USA.

Sweeter than Sweetest Bird
by **Paul Kasobya**

I'm seated under the shade of moon
On this one other of my lonesome nights,
Bewailing the gone influential voiced figure,
A global renaissance feminine bard
A flagpole of undaunted success;
Marguerite Annie Johnson.

Betwixt my heart's wrath and mirth:
Wrath for a great loss to my world
Mirth for the inspiration from her word;
Fingers of mine now betroth this quill
To paint eulogical lines that be
Extolling the immense beauty of a life;
Maya's song, flung up to heaven!

I sing not with my tongue in the cheek,
For every word about her parts my jaws wide.
I either honour such a strugglist
Or whole heartedly praise a realist she was.

Maya winsome Angelou;
How waking dost thy name sound
Yet heartening is a life history of thine!

The bird whose song is sweetest
Uponst a smooth and firm bough sits
And blows its toothless bill.

But how? O should I revoke!

To acclaim you the sweeter than sweetest bird
Who yet sang from precarious shrubs,
But left resounding echoes enough-
To the hearing ear and heart.

Maya multilingual Angelou,
African-American of extreme valour
I delight in your stature!
The startling truth about your nature:
 As a client girl built from the cellar,
A toiling teenage mother with artistic humour
To a salient woman on a tower's hair.

When parity was gone from public eye,
When the black skin was like a devil condemned,
 You gracefully turned plight to pride
Never fleeing your skin but,
You with vitality blew the trumpet
Whose sound of equality threw up the banner of peace
In mother world!

Maya affable Angelou;
Advocate off parley where claws were high,
I admire thy resting shoulder
Which rubbed with Malcom's and Luther's,
Both of whose dreams you witnessed.

Poetic hero, calypso lady
Your unputdownable oeuvre:
I know why the caged bird sings
A song flung up to heaven
On the pulse of the morning

Down in the delta Is,

A brave and startling truth
That fans weary hearts of-
Mom and me and mom
To leave lit
The black candle.

As yourself rests wherever your soul may be
I hammer these lines with rapture in my blood
For a life fulfilling like yours,
Is unique and scarce like it is.
But still in my lungs,
A breath of gratitude is heavy within
And is sent up to you,
A role model whose life story is mentoring me.

The stars are looking down at me
Crossing my fingers, alone on a warm African night,
Muttering my prayer to the most invisible artist
Who paints anew the sky at every dawn;
That your soul he takes
And hoods in a celestial rose land,

Paul Kasobya is a young Ugandan undergraduate, emerging writer and an aspiring author. Co-founder of an upcoming charity organization.

The Invisible Chains
by **Mbenkum Elvis Kinyuy**

From the USA to Africa setting the pace,
Your works echo through time and place.
Articles, poetry and all your plays
Surviving with grace always
Phenomenal artist, phenomenal woman
Forever Maya, forever Angelou

Most honored woman in generations
Awards, honors and many other distinctions
In writing, direction and other professions
A guardian star for many generations
Phenomenal artist, phenomenal woman
Forever Maya, forever Angelou

Honored was the place
That bore such an ace
Now lifted to grace
To her life says
Phenomenal leader, phenomenal woman
Forever Maya, forever Angelou

Mbenkum Elvis Kinyuy is a student and rising Cameroonian poet.

Dancing to the Grave
by **Mafa Maiketso**

I first heard about you when the music was playing
And the dance floor was smoking, and samba was in full
swing
And then the music stopped
There was a hush in space when you were born
The universe realized no music would play again
Until you took to the stage
You came
You danced, the music played, but again, silence

He swindled you out of your innocence
Tearing tissues meant to be fondled only in love and care
Drowning you in darkness where fear and malice reside
Switching music off in your soul, burying you barren in the
land of the dead

And you died
And when you died Maya
Your shoes began to move
You made time to stand and stare
Your destiny became your mystery
Your focus befitted your truth
Your passion became your action
Your hand reached for God
You let go of what could have been
You dressed up in the glow of love
 You rejoiced in the joy of a flower
Basking in the beauty of its essence
...and you danced again Maya

Then I heard birds singing in the forest
But that meant nothing to me
Until I got lost in the music wafting from a bird caged in the
wire
As I dropped everything to listen
There was a sound so soft and so still
Something close to a whisper, close to death
But there were no sobs, nor wailing in the songs issuing
from the bird in the cage
The music harmonized with melodies from beyond the blues
A choir was in session above the stars
I knew Maya was back in her shoes

But now, Maya, your shoes are empty
The floor is quiet, the lights are off, the samba is gone
The pain of losing you endows me with tenderness
Beauty and freedom of healing
Your prettiest smile, I know, held the deepest secrets only
you knew
Your prettiest eyes, I know, have cried the most tears
Your kindest heart, aha, has felt the most pain
Though death leaves a heartache no one can heal Your love
leaves a memory no one can steal

Mafa Maiketso from Lesotho is a male Mosotho, lecturer in Guidance &
Counseling, MA in Education, motivational speaker, writes motivational
columns for magazines and newspapers, writes poetry and short stories
for pleasure

From Dream to Destiny
(In loving memory of Dr. Maya Angelou)
by **Koketso Marishane**

Everybody risks, that's for sure, in all kinds of acts and deeds one performs, there's only one risk one cannot avoid. With solutions to problem cases, one cannot choose a place of rest, in terms of cultures, religions, and customary laws, one gets only one chance to meet one's creator.

With the physical being left untouched and the soul going where it belongs. Having culture made by our elders, religions influenced by leaders (sometimes depending in which continent, country and world one lives in), may perhaps structure one's belief, and having customary laws in the community, might perhaps also anticipate in the decision making.

Thus, being human on this earth, one should always try by all means to reach the ultimate soul satisfaction in terms of religion to avoid pressure.

Churches come in names like colours do, and surely will the information differ from one head to another. Carefulness in thoughts then rise to effective plans to occur, with beliefs so different but leading to one creator. Dreams occurring so ordinary like parents plan for their children so will the dictionaries come in different covers but similar tenses; so I'd say, whether you've believed there's heaven or not, you've entered. The heavenly angels have welcomed you.

You've been sung as the greatest 21st century communicator of our time for none-other neither befits your shoes nor can lift the mountains you moved through your verbal prowess, your mouth emitted magic. Those that ululate your name, from the parley gates of heaven polished by your fellow comrades Es'kia Mphahlele, Chinua Achebe, Bessie Head and other literary institutions that have panelled your deeds still wonder how the future looks, for their paths are still not paved, your being was of a special kind.

Like you've saluted the golden iconic Mandela, your gigantic traits too are still cherished by many, those with hopes and wishes of breathing sheer excellence wherever their names appear, will continue to bow upon admission in your honour at the literary emperors, for your marks are heavenly noted. Those with activated periphery organs are testament of your spirit.

May the worldly ancestors, angels, dreamers and travelers traversing tide peacefully welcome your presence as you join the legendary spirits that guide us. We'll forever honour the grounds you walked on.

Koketso Marishane is an obsessed Arts Education & Information Communications Technology practitioner from GaMarishane in South Africa. He is a servant leader at the Es'kia Mphahlele Trust among other organizations around the world.

Chapter 3

Maya Angelou walks along the beach in San Francisco, 1970.

(© Bettman/CORBIS)

Photo source: http://bit.ly/1I4WY4g

Call Her Maya
by **Ogwo David Emenike**

On the pulse of morning
She rose
Above the stings of yesterday's defeats;
Above the traumas of past mistakes

She knew why the caged bird sings
Thus, like the Nightingale
Beautifully she sang songs of hope
Aspirations springing high to touch the skies

We have gathered together in her name
Singin' and Swingin'
What a beautiful gift to humanity!
A song flung up to heaven

Call her Maya
Her soul forever will soar higher.

Ogwo David Emenike is a Sage, Motivator, Essayist, Poet and Author.
He's a coordinator at Hinovelty, and enjoys reading, writing and thinking.

Epitaph on Maya Angelou
by **Emilly Achieng**

Farewell ye Phenomenal Woman,
Precious gift,
You still rise in our thoughts
Your light dimeth not,
Your skills fadeth not,
Your words still echo; Sleep well,
Phenomenal woman.

Emilly Achieng is from Nairobi, Kenya. She is an avid reader and writer.

With Grace
by **Oloyede Charles Akinropo**

With the rising of the day
To grace I onward gaze
For what I might behold
Undaunted with many plights
A crystal tomorrow I see.

Where cometh thy hope?
With grace I humbly answered
Why shouldn't I dream?
It's the free gift of life
Even in chains or shackles.

Triumph I see
Triumph I have
The grace to live
In the midst of my reality

Pang! pang! the horror came
My jubilant soul silenced
My voice stolen Left without grace
And the song of defeat
I hear within and without

At last my white is turned red
Deprived of my pride

Was it ever pride?
Many voices I hear
Lost without grace

Bound in my soul
tomorrow is bleak
It was only a fantasy
The deprivation of my sanity
Left without grace

Suddenly, I found clarity
Yes! I was violated
Unprotected,untrusted
As darkness engulfed me
Gross darkness that blinded my soul

But a choice I have
Whether to lie in defeat
Or chart my course with grace

Hope surged into my soul
Reviving me from the darkened land
With freshness of possibilities
Grace was restored to me
My choice is what matters

A decision I made
One which the world would know
My voice they would hear
Vibrating into the hearts of men
With grace I would live
Not anymore without grace

My best I would give

And become all I could be
With grace I would triumph
Showing others how
Grace has found me after all
And in good faith I would give myself to mankind!

Oloyede Charles Akinropo is a young leadership student, coach and writer

She Sings Her Pain Away
by **Victoria Siphiwe Mamvura-Gava**

The only place she feels permitted
Taking a Shower, Cooking or Cleaning
The Place Bathroom or Kitchen
The African Woman Cooks & Cleans
For that she has to be Clean & Allowed to Sing
Given two places to be
Her only Liberty Avenue
That is where she sings for a Revolution
She believes now - is the time for a New Revolution
The greatest of them All – giving herself to receive
Helping a Friend and a Stranger in Need – She Sings her Pain
Away

Victoria Siphiwe Mamvura-Gava MPhil; PDM; MDHR; Assoc BMgt; ADR; NVC CfE; DipPTM; Accredited Assessor & Moderator Services SETA; IntDip ICSA is a Zimbabwean born woman of substance. She is a member of Alchemy Deluxe and Mamvura InterTrades

You Want to Know Who I Am
by **Trinisa M. Pitts**

It takes some inner soul searching and history to figure out
Who I am.
It takes the ability to go beyond what everyone else can see
The Charisma and style that shows from deep within how
could that be.

Isn't it true that what is on the inside will show up on the
outside? Then why ask why not wait
The time will come that everyone will know that the Legacy I
bring, sings melodies for journey's to come

You want to know who I am? This woman that everyone
says is an icon, who is she?

Could this be me? The poetic person that has such a flow.
Take a guess or a gander.

Aren't you Curious? Don't you want to know? What strong
Black talented woman that everyone thinks is so great and
to some they can even relate. I am only pushing for what I
believe, what God has instilled inside of me that is Who I AM
and who I continued to be. For decades, and hours in a day. I
only portrayed to be who I felt was inside of me. I never lost
myself to anyone else.

I continued to be strong and knew the place where I belonged. It was in a spiritual realm that kept me in my inner peace. God was my source and made me see all that I gathered and all that I embraced would be locked away in a place, for a time such as this when everyone would like to know what I was made of and wanted to know Who I am.

I already know who I am. I am me. A phenomenal woman with a track record of not only success but the best left Legacy because I believed In God and I believed in myself. You want to know who I am Maya Angelou.

Trinisa M. Pitts Author, Poet and Motivational speaker helps those struggling with overwhelming challenges in life by sharing her past personal testimony that is now filled with, purpose and The Divine.

MAYA ANGELOU
by **Kealeboga mosekiemang**

Maya, mama, mother of poetry
Alas! Mother of creation, the model of beautiful
Your love as deep as a bone marrow
A bright star that shone on us, who taught me to stand that
heat
And bear the cold
Nobody here, nobody there can erase you, for you are a
Goddess painted permanently in the museum of my heart
Extraordinary you are, for you said
Life does go on, it will be better tomorrow, for
Our poet, Maya, my poem, she could make you cry and
smile at the same time
Unique like an undisturbed pond: MAYA, MAMA, ANGEL OF
POETRY.

Kealeboga mosekiemang is a gifted poet based in Gaborone Botswana, Africa. He has been a performer since 1997, open mic shows, presidential activities and other shows for example, Gaborone 2014. He loves writing poetry, short stories and also do theater shows. Maya was one phenomenal woman whom he got some of his inspirations from.

Spring and Shine
by **Eric Kombey Wolete**

You woman, you little woman!
Don't you know how to spring?
What are you still doing in the wilderness?
Come on you woman, you little girl!
Stand; stand up, with the arm of Maya;
Stand and spring, and spring with honour,
And honour the colour of favour.

You woman, you little descendant!
Don't you know it's time to shine?
Why are you still sleeping and nosing?
Won't you wake up for the mass?
The bell is ringing and the choir singing
Won't you wake up and burn like fire,
Or and spring and shine like Maya!

You glowing light, little East-West woman!
Won't you shine on the face of Maya,
And keep her fame burning and shinning?
Won't you sing her song and dance her dance,
And play the rumba, salsa and pachanga?
You woman, don't you know you're a rock!
Arise and shine, and shine for Maya.

Eric Kombey Wolete is a Cameroonian. He holds a Post Graduate
Diploma in Sociology. This doyen is a Consultant, Administrative and
Financial Unit at Central Hospital, Yaoundé-Cameroon.

Tribute to Maya Angelou
by **Olamide Oderinlo**

The world stood still to hear you say those words
The earth wanted a part of you too
Those words forever locked in a zillion waves
The earth forever enchanted by your cosy strides.

You lived a million years away
You saw more than the world around you
You lived the future today
Your visions brought the dreams to live.

When many left their visions ashore
When the storms of life raged ravenously
When the waters eroded their thoughts
Through the storms you lived your life.

Many lives you touched and changed
Many dreams you aided to life
Many lived because you could
Many dared because you did too.

A black African child writes
In the wake of the morning
She writes about your life inspired
She would write and write and again write.

Olamide Oderinlo is a cultural resource management activist, a passionate writer and a prolific motivational speaker. She holds a bachelors degree in archaeology and a master's degree in tourism development both from the University of Ibadan. Her main passion and motivation is the sustainable development of the human society and women empowerment.

A Goal Oriented woman
by **Ralph Llyod**

Her eyes sparkle like a bright star in the sky.
She has the stamina, beauty, and courage that one would admire,
Even the love and happiness one inspires It ought to make you proud.
She is a woman that one can always count on, and a woman that sees no wrong.

Her beauty shines from the inside out,
Her smile shines beautifully like the sun rising over the horizon, and her intelligence, wisdom, and hard work are not surprising. She is a genuinely caring women who goes the extra mile to help one in need or broken hearted, and throughout all of her hard work, no one ever sees her fall apart.

You were always there to protect me through the dark and cold of night
We would pretend we're in another
She said that she'd changed
On a journey for her gnosis.
Was this a real spiritual walk?

Ralph Llyod from Monrovia, Liberia, West Africa holds a degree in Computer Science. He is a Christian.

She Lives On
by **Ajise Vincent**

A paragon of virtue
A voice of time
A dame with masculine virtue
Reposed in gleeful prime

A medieval citadel coated in modern swagger
Spuring the goodies of the past into the present found
She stood against gender chauvinism with stern raga
And doused erroneous political propagandas that abound

With her gray hair of insight
She swept the literary world
Till they through her had foresight
To impact the universe with word(s)

In bravery she stared death in the eye
Jagging the gruesome art of racism
Till in glee it bid bye
Giving way to welfarism

With her quill of splendour
She broadcasted the message of peace
To war torn countries that bore,
Till the war was killed by her ink grease

Lo, death vanishes her softening
Ay, the shadow of time trigger its gun
Her words are forever in the offing
For in our hearts, they live on

Ajise Vincent is an Economics Undergraduate at the Federal University of Agriculture Abeokuta, Nigeria. He greatly loves Maya Angelou and will forever propel her doctrines till time memorial.

Chapter 4

Maya Angelou reads her poem, *"On the Pulse of the Morning,"* at the inauguration of President William Jefferson "Bill" Clinton, 1993.

(© Reuters/CORBIS)

Photo source: http://bit.ly/1OleZQJ

The Star that Shines
by **Malgu Seebaway**

Hail that phenomenal woman whose words touched the
heart of the stone heart
That nightingale whose sweet melody tamed the ferocious
lion.
Grace to her personality
As she walked her gentle paces
She gained her respect
While she taught peace
 She shook hands with unity
Embracing every soul in her abode
She was no other than a woman
A phenomenal woman.

She alone sat with the queen
And dined with the royals
Like she possessed royalty
Oh yes! She was a queen on her own
A phenomenal woman indeed.

That phenomenal woman
An African beauty, brightens the night skies of Africa.
Twinkles much more than wet diamond
And inspired man's fruitful offspring
She is a victor and also victorised
She's much more than uttered words
She's a phenomenal woman

Long live Maya Angelou

Long live all women
The phenomenal woman.

Malgu Seebaway lives in Accra, Ghana. Student of T.I. Ahmadiyya
Secondary School kumasi, Ghana. Father is Sheikh Seebaway Zakaria, an
Islamic Scholar and lecturer at Kwame Nkrumah University of Science
and Technology. Mother is Habibah Sohuah, a seamstress.

Your Crown
by **Mmakgosi Ophadile Anita Tau**

I want to be your crown one day,
when in maturity we seek stability,
an ornament of elegance, substance and influence that sits
on your head,
the pride in your backbone as you walk,

I will to make you a handsome king amongst men,
for my lips never mention loud talk that is empty and vile,
it overflows of truth and wisdom our forefathers were in
search of,
the brilliance within will glitter each time you wear me,

Divine love will be reflected in every word I say,
your friends will seek my insight,
yet never dare to ask for it,
everywhere I go gracious truths will follow me,
spring in unending glory from this woman,

I will comfort you,
when heavy rains raise hell in our home,
I will heal you,
as the bone of your bone,
coordinate wellness within us,
such that peace may locate your heart,

In unison we will overthrow defeat,
it will never conceal our hearts,
or burn out our flame, as long as you wear me,
the crown of prosperity will never leave you.

Mmakgosi Ophadile Anita Tau is a living testimony from Botswana, an inspiration and an author of four mobile poetry applications and an e-book titled, '*All Over My Tswana Mind.*'

Woman of Substance
by **Liketso Ramafikeng**

Blossoming like vines spreading their fragrance is her presence,
her presence more delighter than wine.
Her love is like a sweet perfume sprayed all over the universe, embracing and welcoming it is to the world.
She is more precious than jewels,
a lily of the valley, and the lily among thorns.
Phenomenal, she is.

Through life she has sailed.
Weathering the tornados and hurricanes life gesticulated at her.
Yet with the brightest smile she shouldered the world.
Her fate, she awaits with no regrets.
She is a tree of life;
she spreads her branches to house all those who hold onto her.
Lay hold on her, like the stars hold onto the moon, for her love is as majestic as her power.
 From the moon and back she would walk to shield her beloved. Phenomenal, she is.

Wrinkles and grey hair is the fountain of wisdom and strength, a manual for endurance and fortitude.
She is no stranger to animosity and adversity but her heart cannot think of a better devotion than the love for her children.
An atonement that overshadows the tribulations encountered. Phenomenal, she is.

A treasure to heaven, but on earth, her life is a ransom to many.
For she constantly strives to aid those captivated by human idiosyncrasies.
A woman who smiles even when her heart is shattered.
A woman of substance.
The true definition of a phenomenal woman, she is.

Liketso Ramafikeng is a visionary young woman and student at the National University of Lesotho, studying economics minor in statistics. She is a poet and a member of Rotaract club (Rotary International).

Mayic Evocation
by **Michael Olusegun Babajide**

Prefix:
MAYA
The masque of your songs
Is not for uninitiated tongues
The reggae of your poetry
Is not for fake feet
The Masquerades of your chorus
Can't be staged in novice dance halls
The beat of your poems
Are too alien to inept legs
Thought for thought
Line like line
Song similar song
I wish to sing to Maya
For Maya the phenomenal woman
With phenomenal poems
Built for her
Phenomenally ...

Appearances:
I am Yoruba
Michael of southwest
Babajide of budding thirst
Of southwest Nigeria
In Southwest Africa
With black lights
Of black times
Searching for my art
In this fiendish life
And in the ritual of Yoruba style

Let me start my iba
With the invocations of incantations:

Ewi	*It is Poetry*
Lonikomaajemini	*That says you must always*
answer me	
Hohohoho	*hohohoho*
Orikiijuba	*Praise poetry*
Lonikimaakioo	*tells me to eulogize you*
Ni dansakidansaki	*with royal renders.*
Sisesise	*Always Amen Always Amen;*
Nitillakoseoo	*Such is Ilakose's*
Maya, mope o nitemi	*Maya, I take my turn today to*
call on you	
lonioooo	
Sara tete, tarashasha	*Be quick, be eager to answer*
Je koju mi sheyooo	*May I do mine successfully*

Body:
Having danced round
Round and round ijuba
May I now proceed to hail Maya
Maya, oya, arise !
A rai a iz !!
A araaaaaaaaaiz !!!
This poem is written for you
After you and for you
This poem is written not for:
    "the fire in my eyes,
      And the flash of my teeth,
       The swing in my waist,
     And the joy in my feet".
For I am a man,
poetically

poetical man
So am I
So as well,
This poem is overwhelmed by
    "The clothes to mend
      The floor to mop
      The food to shop
      Then the chicken to fry
      The baby to dry
company to feed
    The garden to weed
shirts to press
The tots to dress
The can to be cut
clean up this hut
see about the sick
And the cotton to pick".

Maya may I
Un-die the "Weekend Glory"
And make it glow daily
Maya may I
Know why the cage bird sings
    "with a fearful trill
of things unknown   ...
Still
    "longed for still
and his tune is heard
on the distant hill ?"...

Suffix:
Freedom bird
Freedom dead
Freedom buried

Freedom with the dead
Freedom for the dead
Freedom from the dead
Freedom from death
Freedom from hell
And in freedom, freedom dwells
And with this angry anthem
In the den of death
And with this flying flag
Of rainbow flags
And with this rousing voice
Daring demi gods
Maya- I now kiss you bye bye
Boastful
                    And
Boastful
That hell will become well when you visit there
And heaven will continue your biography before I get there

Postscript:
Life is when death is absent
The absence of life is death
The absence of death is life

Michael Olusegun Babajide is a "Yoruba boy" of Southwest Nigeria. He is a lover of all genres of Literature with a deep yearning for fostering his creative feelings.

Becoming Me
by **Zainab Kakal**

I was asked to settle,
Adjust, adapt and compromise;
Simply because I was born a woman
with a hundred million ties.

I do not complain,
I find it brave to be,
all these women
expected as per your decree.

Now, I have years of practice
of being her, her and her.
Each one strong and sharp
doing what you hold dear.

You did a fine job, I say,
of controlling and instructing me.
But, lately, I feel like a birthing force
waiting to be set free.

I am now a power unforeseen,
And you have yourself to blame.
You made me bigger and better by giving me so many
names.

I am beyond myself;
Every wall is tearing down,
I am a woman with many faces each one I call my own.

Zainab Kakal is an Indian into sustainable development, tourism and social entrepreneurship. She is a yoga enthusiast, a published writer and has travelled to 30 countries, most of them solo.

Wake up
by **Elizabeth Ayoola**

Wake up! Wake up and keep me company.
Everything reminds me of you;
The way my sheets cling to my skin,
The way my hair lays tangled on the pillow like our bodies in
bliss.
Your scent; the way it lingers in the air telling stories of a
love half lived,
A door half open and two hearts half closed.

Wake up! Wake up and keep me company,
King of my nights and master of my dreams,
Every image that forms when I close my eyes is made from
you,
Birthed from you, ignited by you,
Consumed in your fire and conceived by you.

Wake up! Wake up and keep me company,
Be my anomaly, my petal that falls from the tree,
When every other petal clings lifelessly to the branches.
Wake up and be the white that cuts through the darkest
black,
Be the beauty that revels in the midst of ashes.

Wake up! Wake up and keep me company,
As I dance on the sun as it rises,
As I search the heart of the moon to understand the mystery
of its surprises.
Keep me company while I hold hands with starfish and give
my heart to the stars.

Wake up and accompany me,
as I search for love in fields,
And bury my treasure in the depths of its grounds,
Help me find God in the harvests,
And find his absence in the dry air of the desserts.

I look for hope in wells,
see your reflection in its waters,
See your life in the withering of tulips,
And feel your love in the floods cleansing my soul.
Wake up and swim with me,
Swim with me in the oceans of my pain,
Wake up and drown with me in the realities of my fantasies.

Elizabeth Ayoola is a spoken word artist and creative writer who has been writing poems and performing for 8 years. She enjoys addressing social issues from a personal perspective.

Mama Angelou
by **Thabo Moloi**

In heavy rains, stormy days
Troubled winds
She woke up, mama took the walk
Along the isolated paths
Tired and exhausted
She never stopped
She kept believing
Her words stood affirm She said
"Nothing will work unless you do"
Her strength was that of a slave
Dedicated as an oppressed mind
Fighting for freedom
A caged bird learnt to sing
Long gone are those days Mama is a Queen.

Thabo Moloi is from South Africa currently residing in Bloemfontein.

The Hero's Farewell
by **Ngoanannete David Lekhanya**

Pardon me the departed soul
You that hath toiled your presence to mark
And thou art of theft mastered
Stealing many a heart
From this world of agony and rage
Where peace is just a talk of day
Whose fate is difficult to maintain
Yet simple to destroy.

This sun is that which once shone
High above your head
For eighty something years of your life
Now we see it below our feet still
While you better see it now
Upon your heart and eyes
Where it now rests
For you to enjoy it more
In your permanent sleep.

Motionless now as you
 lie In your glamorous box
Damn grieving coffin I mean
You own your pair of ears still
With which you listen no more
To our cries and comments
But enjoy the height above our heads
Through the desolate village   .
Where you shall rest in peace.

This world you so timeously left
Is full of terrible troubles
Mischievous acts and brutalities
Man-made storms and disasters
From which we cease not to cry
You shall cry no more
You shall hear no more
For you crowned with an endless smile
And journeyed through the earth' stomach
There to meet your creator
And enjoy eternal peace
Rest in peace...rest in peace.

Ngoanannete David Lekhanya, a Mosotho Male Assistant lecturer in Social and Development studies BED in English Language and Development studies He derives pleasure in writing poetry and children's stories.

A Phenomenal Bud
by **Tigele Nlebesi**

1. A little girl with crepe hands, slicked desperately in cocoa
butter
Food for the gaping lips, of hungry skin
So much malaise.
Such a little girl body to carry it
An arid mouth
The war within a little girl body
And the one without
Leaves bones picked clean
Flesh cracked open.
So much empty.
No room for love

2. She breaks the spine of a long forgotten holy book
Packed away in kuku's box with her other yesterdays
"I know why the caged bird sings"
The title tremolandos in the hollow of that little girl body
The pages feel like skin torn from her own hands
A light comes on. Some sense of belonging
She reads your words.
Savours them like sunlight at dusk
Pulls them in between her teeth like oil
Presses them against her lonely palate
Glazes them on her lips like honey
Once, twice, thrice over
A light goes off.
Something painful flees the body

3. You should be here to see
The bloom you cultivate from the hard earth of a little girl
mouth
The magic you etch into every crease in her skin
The sudden swell in her voice
The new pair of eyes
The smile of her body
The light that comes on
And the one that goes off
You should be here to see
She is yours
The tender bud of a phenomenal woman

*Kuku is a Kalanga word for grandmother

Tigele Nlebesi is a Kalanga University of Botswana student. He works at a local girl's empowerment magazine Sky and charity organization, Men and Boys for Gender equality, special focus on women's rights.

Rendezvous with Excellence
by **Sigeh Leonard Lenjo**

Maya, I know where we will meet.
I choose not to seduce you last night.
I could not ask for your crafty hand
In the heart of that sophistry award,
There male drummers played with noise.

Back home I did not sleep till dawn.
I turned, and teased your brave pages.
Your sweet voice drained through my heart.
It chilled me like tender fresh dew.
Dew freshly freed from last night.

Up south in my enclave homeland-
Far from the reach of an Arian race,
Where neither class, nor sexism can reach;
On the Empyrean of my lonely wit,
I listened to a lonely wind's sweet tune.

The enclave virginity of your voice-
Where seraphs serve authentic muse,
Where you were culturally born and breath,
Where on an ancient colored tapestry
Avant-garde sages ushered your steps.

Where you stroll with shooting stars-
Where the circled moon dates with you,
A spot that is never forgotten,
A voice that cannot be mistaken;
On the Magnus Opus of lives-

Where I will meet queens and heroines-
Where queens and heroines will meet me;
There on the eternal musedom,
There I will raise my lowered cup
And taste your Female bass.

Sigeh Leonard Lenjo is a Cameroonian with B.A degree in Modern Letters. He is champing on getting his Poetry collection entitled 'Soul of Storm' published.

Chapter 5

Maya Angelou

Photo source: http://bit.ly/1bBmmlM

Beatification for Maya Angelou
by **Oyin Oludipe**

With earth, soul-head reckons soon!
When grim sailcloth hoists our tongues on laps
Of time, yielding ours to fertile rites

Not in storm, but in leap impervious
To thorns of grain, mortal dirge
And gift-reins of the feeble

The world stows in tidal waves,
Prowls to stranglehold of light
Sprung from your grace

So now you are no season, no morbid stalk
Marking currents of time, but maw
To spew new worlds

So stay you light on this mangled shoot,
Kernel bridge, spun beyond all essence
A vagrant dance stirs upon

A child's hermit glimpse.
Stay you glad echoes of the infant rites,
You are navel to this gorge.

Oyin Oludipe is a Nigerian playwright and editor. His works have been published on Kaneem and The New Black Magazine, the Guardian Newspaper and others

Phenomenally Woman
by **Rubaba Mohammed**

They cannot fathom my strength
Flat chest and broad shoulders, no way
My clenched fist could not harm a fly
My voice; it is hoarse less
Let the wind blow and I am carried along
I cannot balance an empty scale
It weighs me down
My fragile face
My feeble feet
My timid tendencies
Take care as you handle her
Be cautions, be careful
My maintainers are foretold
Strength could not be my possession
Yet I am a woman; strong
A woman; phenomenal
Phenomenal woman; I am
Strength; I am strong
It is not in the shine of my eyeballs
But in the shades of my gaze
It is not in the name of my gender
But in the spirit and soul of this life
It is never in the sound of my voice
But in my unabated uttering
It is neither in my height nor weight
No, it is not in the colour of my skin
It is not in the hugeness of my muscles
It is in the build of my brain
The mould of my mind

It is in the heat of this heart
Because I am a woman, phenomenal
I am a woman; strong
My anger terrifies thunder
Yet my smile shines the sun
Talk to me but be mild
For my words stab the dragons dead
Yet to my love the doves come
My warmness calms volcanoes
To the seas my sweetness dictates the waves
It is in the flow of this garment
The feel of my veil
The gift of my Love
Phenomenally a phenomenal woman

Rubaba Mohammed is a graduate of University of Ghana with BSc in Agric. (Agribusiness), a playwright, a poet and an author. He loves and gains wisdom from reading, writing, watching and listening.

Phenomenal, Indeed
by **Kearoma Desiree Mosata**

The truth is I was very hesitant to write this essay because my mind still doesn't want to believe that Dr. Maya Angelou is no longer with us.
She was and still is my role model and I have always built up these scenarios that one day I would meet her. We would sit and talk about her writing and my writing and she would tell me stories about growing up with her grandmother and I too would tell her about mine who gave me the first Maya Angelou literary work I read which was *I Know Why The Caged Bird Sings*.

n my writer's mind which has no trouble conjuring up scenarios, we would sit under a morula tree and drink Rooibos tea and she would laugh in her deep throaty voice as she tells me about her stay in Ghana, the first time she read A Tale Of Two Cities and what she thought of it and I would tell her about growing up in Botswana although it really isn't all that exciting as her life.

I read I Know Why The Caged Bird Sings because it had been a gift and as a teenager I wasn't very much into biographies but I enjoyed reading classics and I put Maya's book as a classic and read on. I was amazed to say the least and was very excited to read more about this phenomenal woman. No one can argue this fact that Maya Angelou was indeed phenomenal. I remember at one point I saw her on Sesame Street and my love for her skyrocketed because Miss Maya was that amazing.

In senior school by virtue of my love for literature I chose English Literature as a subject and to my great joy the first poem we studied was *Still I Rise* and it took me about an hour to read it, analyze it and then decide that yes Maya Angelou was a superwoman whose work made me want to wear a red cape and conquer the world as she was doing. I remember coming home very excited and not even the rain or grey clouds could kill my happiness. I then looked up Maya's other poems and to this day I cannot exactly pinpoint my favorite poem because all her work leaves me starry eyed with either great fascination or sadness and sometimes both because she has this way with words that makes one feel, yes her work makes one feel all the emotions she's trying to get across. If she had ever wrote about how marvelous avocados are, even though I hate them I bet I would possibly consider liking them because she made them sound great.

Phenomenal woman however is one poem I think every young woman must read in her teens not because I love it and its writer but as I have been a young black teenager (some might say I still am one) I have experienced what every young black teenage girl experiences in fact what every young teenage girl faces. Lack of confidence, lack of self-esteem, the great terrors of peer pressure and I have looked down upon myself because of all these and felt that somehow I wasn't good enough to become anything/anyone noteworthy in society. *Phenomenal Woman* and *Still I Rise* talk of someone, a woman who has no doubt in herself and her abilities and who soldiers on through whatever storm and whatever life throws at her.

A phenomenal woman always has her head held up high and is not shot down with words, looks or any other minor thing. As a feminist in the twenty first century, a lot of things happening to the youth make me very sad. The Nigerian students (The Chibok School Girls) for instance have been abducted for over months and still it seems their mothers will sleep on tear stained pillows worrying to death about their daughters. This travesty and many others happening not just in Africa to young woman need urgent attention and my essay on Maya Angelou might not do much but at least I am putting it out there.

I wrote the poem (Young Black Girl) below not just in honor of Dr. Maya Angelou but in honor of every woman, young or old who is going through something, it might not be a huge tragedy, it might be family disputes, it might be school problems and it might be something heart wrenching like abuse, poverty, wars and political unrest but this poem is for every young black girl out there.

Young Black Girl

Starry eyes that resemble the map of Africa
Great Africa land of my forefathers
My forefathers who brought me into this great Africa

Great Africa where I reside
Great Africa where black is always beautiful and radiant.
Great Africa where my tears and cries are heard from far across the sea

My tears fall on this great African soil,

African soil whose color resembles my skin
My skin that's been subjected to the harsh whips of life

And these scars I bear on my skin a sure sign of the pains of
being a young black girl
And these tears a true sign of the hardships I have endured
and am still enduring and will
Endure till time infinite
Because when God made me, he decided to make me walk
on fires barefoot
He made me to walk in thunderstorms
And war zones unarmed

But I am a soldier
A great African soldier
I am a melanin goddess ordained for great things

The sun rises and sets each day
And my dreams grow with each sunset
And with each sunrise I wear my cape,
My great African cape made of animal skin, sweat, tenacity
and the great African spirit

Because I am a young black girl
I am a young black soldier
And soldier on I shall.

Kearoma Desiree Mosata is a poet and writer in Botswana, studying
Applied Sciences. She writes and do poetry shows. Maya Angelou was a
great role model to her and she still is.

Letter to Death
by **Idowu Joshua**

I didn't believe death has no respect
Until I heard she has gone to rest
My heart is sorrowful
Painful, she left without saying goodbye
Death why have you kept our hero far away from us
My heart is clamoring
Seeking for one more life chance
Death took away the woman of life
Am left with the moon light at night
No more story about life at the moon time
But her words keeps bleeding in my heart
She is an inspiration to my aspiration
My mind is filled with jubilation
Whenever I read of her remarkable dedication
Which keeps giving me hope of reaching the sky
MAYA ANGELOU
I couldn't change the covenant with death
But your memories live in my heart ever
Which keeps you living forever
Rest in peace!

Idowu Joshua from Ekiti State loves drawing and writing. He lives in Ibadan, studied Education in Oyo college of Education, Nigeria. He is known on social media as Esoterik Joshua

Woman
by **Dumiso Gatsha**

Woman. The backbone in which change is defined and
adopted.
Woman. The strength in which a family is sustained.
Woman. A signal of virtue embalmed in the crest of a
morning's horizon.
I look to a mother for wisdom abundant,
Passed down through generations of survival and at times,
emancipation.
I look to a young lady to see Africa's future,
Tipped above trendy heels and relayed in ethnic speech.
I look to the cornerstone of love,
The pioneers of resilience and patience.
The world knows no good with no phenomena of grace,
The young know no better with no nurturing embrace,
Great is she who's a part of society,
Great is she who understands femininity.
For the universe is only fabulous, when she smiles with
dignity.

Dumiso Gatsha is an MSc Scholar, Equality Activist, Finance Professional
and Youth Catalyst in issues of Education, Sexual Reproductive Health &
Rights and Youth from Botswana

The Poet
by **Maphehelle Mokete**

Imagine the poet as a madwoman.
Draw analogous lunacy.
Ban, Curse and call her whatever name.
Think you that she seeks fame.
Gather all wits, look into the sky,
And behold with your naked eye.
The moon offers her light,
And flashes it upon midnight.
Through the selfish clouds she paves her way
To shame darkness away
She kisses the earth, oceans tremble
Shadows grow larger than the highest temple
That light is the poet's voice,
To whose drumbeat we must dance.
Before she disappears just as the moon does
When we wish she was still with us.

Maphehelle Mokete, a Mosotho man, is a lecturer in English language
and literature at the Lesotho College of Education.

A wonderful Woman
by **Ipinlaye Oluwakamiye Phebe**

Not just a woman more like a man
Who exudes superiority,
yet eschews inferiority,
Whose grace displayed maturity,
Whose voice sung the unity in diversity,
Swam through life hurdles,
Playing her part in the struggle
A Phenomenal Woman.

Ipinlaye Oluwakamiye Phebe is a young Nigerian undergraduate,
emerging writer and difference maker.

Doleful Melody
by **Bismark Seth Opoku**

Once again an ominous sting
Has bedeviled the fabric of our existence;
It's mark has deeply been felt.
For it has brought a loss
We can never be recompensed for.
The weaver of gripping expressions
Interspersed with beauty of emotions and inspiration
Has been withdrawn from our land of orbiting evanescence
To the shores of eternity
Where life exists in a tranced reality of immortality.

I know why the caged bird sings no more;
 It is now time for echoes of her songs
To ripple with perpetuity through history.
That phenomenal woman who groomed her
Has freed her from mortality's captivity.
Let lovers of all the lore
She inscribed on tablets of remembrance
With the trail of her steps and artistry of her palms
Forget not to keep rising in synchrony with her legacy.

The eve of Maya's leave-taking
Was never a forerunner of a dawn of mourning.
Let the living erect statutes in salutation to her rectitude.

Felicity has vacated our tents,
For reason of her sudden absence.
Yet it left us with an undying season

In which to celebrate the parting of another valorous soul
Who now lives forever to die no more.

Bismark Seth Opoku, popularly known on social media and arts world as
'Seth Boss Kay, is a Ghanaian poet. He graduated from the University of
Ghana with a Bachelor of Arts degree in Psychology and Information
Studies.

My Mama
by **Habib Akewusola**

You are exclusive,
Been my passage from birth to earth.
I cherish your strength to every length.
Throughout infant,
You were my tent.
Am now sensible
But still your pet.
I wish you good health
With lots of wealth,
I have never compromised your love for me.
In time of test
You were the best.
I know you are God-sent.
When am in doubts
You are always at hand
To give me facts.
Mama you are my air,
I will love you till the end.

Habib Akewusola is a published Poet and a student of University of Ilorin.

Grandmothers and How We Ache to Lose Them
by **Nomonde Ndwalaza**

American poet and author Maya Angelou passed away when she was 86. As an admirer of her work the expedient thing to do might have been to mentally prepare myself for her imminent death, especially because she had lived a life truly worth writing about -she'd seen a number of things, felt a lot, and her politics were relatable enough to be universally relevant. And yet, the news of her death left me shocked and saddened. Shocked because death, although inevitable, is perpetually disarming. And rather than be perpetually paranoid, we relegate its permanence to the back of our minds and go about our days with the numbing illusion that we have time. Suddenly, memories of her work – from the books to the quotes to the poetry, all came back, in rapid succession. I became sad because I remembered how she had made me feel.

I was in grade 11 when I first engaged with Maya's work. My best friend lent me a copy of " I know why the Caged Bird Sings" and I remember giggling myself silly in the train while reading a scene about a character's rigid determination to get the pastor to 'Preach it!'. I would read on, in total admiration of Maya' s life, and her propensity to take stock of her whatever her current situation was, and not be afraid to pack her bags and pursue happiness wherever she felt it would be found. Maya, a sensitively imaginative writer who knew the limits of language and the possibilities of silence, made the reader understand and empathize with the difficultly of being little black girl caught up in the process of becoming in a world that is harsh and unkind. I loved how she loved her brother Bailey, and how his love and affirmation of her allowed her to grow into a person that would gleefully welcome all the gifts that life has to give. In speaking about her brother in the book, she says "Of all the needs (there are none imaginary) a lonely child has, the one that must be satisfied, if there is going to be hope and a hope of wholeness, is the unshakable need for an unshakable God. My little Black brother Bailey was my Kingdom Come." To this day, the level of love in this quote still makes my heart smile.

The world, and specifically black girls and women, have lost one of their grandmothers. A woman who made us understand that we are special and kind and important and that our bodies, as big, small, plumpy and complex as they are, are phenomenal. In a world where black life is tough and being a black woman is taxing, where it's important for us to learn our lessons and to learn them quickly; it is the Maya Angelou's of the world who taught us to be doubly armed and doubly prepared. Maya shouted "black child, it's possible" long before lovely Lupita Nyongo came along and reminded us that our dreams are valid.

This sense of sadness that I feel is familiar. It's similar to the emotional desolation that I felt when Whitney Houston and Lebo Mathosa and more recently, Gabriel Garcia Marquez died. I had never met these people and I probably never would have, but they did touch me in some way, whether it was to come into my dark mind a light a fuse that's been burning ever since , or tug at my heart strings and make me contemplate life on frigid Friday night. And it's the issues they argued for, the questions they questioned that makes me remember it all.

So as my peers and I gather in collective grief to reflect on Maya and who she is to us, as we remember just how amazing this woman is, we are reminded of how she inspired us to show up for life, to be better and do better, and to take no prisoners in our quest to be self definitive self actualisers and quintessential badasses.
RIP Mama Maya.

Nomonde Ndwalaza is a radio content producer from South Africa. He enjoys reading, writing, singing, dancing and contemplating life.

Creditude
by **Ifeanyi Enoch Onuoha**

Blessed are you for upholding peace,
You shall forever enjoy bliss.

Blessed are you for overcoming pain,
It's now humanity's gain.

Blessed are you for being a voice,
It taught us not to be noise.

Blessed are you for your writing,
To human minds it's enlightening.

Blessed are you for being a phenomenal woman,
You have inspired in men reason to honor women.

Blessed are you for being a shero,
To us you are now a mirror.

Blessed are you for being uncaged,
You have caused us to be saved.

Blessed are you for living a purpose-driven life,
In God's bosom shall your abode be.

You are a treasure,
We love you dear Angel Maya!

Ifeanyi Enoch Onuoha is a young African leader initiating ways for human betterment. He is a leader at Hinovelty, transformational writer, inspirational speaker, published author and social entrepreneur.

Goodbye Maya
by **Paul Abiola Oku-ola**

And so her pen takes a deep sleep
Never again to undertake any ride
But the written cuts really deep
Never to be forgotten on this divide
Goodbye Maya!

Paul Abiola Oku-ola (pauldesimple) is a Nigerian poet and playwright.

Chapter 6

Maya Angelou

Photo source: http://bit.ly/1PvRBNr

In Maya's Word
Quotes of Dr. Maya Angelou

1. I will not be ashamed. I will not be misused, not willingly. But I will be of use; anybody who is not of use is useless.

2. My mission in life is not merely to survive, but to thrive; and so with passion, some compassion, some humor, and some style.

3. Success is liking yourself, liking what you do, and liking how you do it.

4. When you learn, teach. When you get, give.

5. The desire to reach the stars is ambitious. The desire to reach hearts is wise.

6. Courage is the most important of all virtues because without courage, you can't practice any other virtue consistently.

7. There is no greater agony than bearing an untold story inside you.

8. I don't trust people who don't love themselves and tell me, 'I love you.' There is an African saying which is: be careful when a naked person offers you shirt.

9. A woman's heart should be so hidden in God that a man has to seek Him just to find her.

10. Try to be a rainbow in someone's life.

11. Listen to yourself and in that quietude you might hear the voice of God.

12. The love of a family, the love of the person can heal. It heals the scars left by a larger society. A massive, larger society.

13. Nothing will work unless you do.

14. When we decide to be happy, we accept the responsibility to bring happiness to someone else.

15. It's one of the greatest gifts you can give yourself, to forgive. Forgive everybody.

16. I've learned that people will forget what you said, people will forget what you did, but people will never forget how you made them feel.

17. You can only become truly accomplished at something you love. Don't make money your goal. Instead pursue the things you love doing and then do them so well that people can't take their eyes off you.

18. My mother said I must always be intolerant of ignorance but understanding of illiteracy. That some people, unable to go to school, were more educated and more intelligent than college professors.

19. The idea of overcoming is always fascinating to me, because few of us realize how much energy we have expended just to be here today.

20. Dignity really means that I deserve the best treatment I can receive, that I have the responsibility to give the best treatment to others.

21. Have enough courage to love.

22. When great souls die, after a period peace blooms, slowly and always irregularly. Spaces fill with a kind of soothing electric vibration. Our senses, restored, never to be the same, whisper to us. They existed. They existed. We can bd. Be and be better. For they existed.

23. I can be changed by what happens to me. But I refuse to be reduced by it.

24. Everything in the universe has rhythm, everything dances.

25. You may shoot me with your words, you may cut me with your eyes, you may kill me with your hatefulness, but still, like air, I'll rise.

26. All great artists draw from the same resource: the human heart, which tells that we are all more alike than we are unalike.

27. If you are trying to be normal, you will never know how amazing you can be.

28. I did then what I know how to do. Now that I know better, I do better.

29. Nothing can dim the light which shines from within.

30. My wish for you is that you continue. Continue to be who and how you are, to astonish a mean world with your act of kindness.

Contact Us

Facebook: www.facebook.com/hinovelty

Twitter: www.twitter.com/hinovelty

Website: www.hinovelty.wordpress.com

Email: www.hinovelty1@gmail.com

Phone Numbers: +2348037633034,
+2347036466412

Made in United States
North Haven, CT
21 September 2022

24408503R00075